The Story

THE DISCO...

T. Rex

Author
DOUGAL DIXON

Barnum Brown *Barnum Brown began his career as a palaeontologist at the American Museum of Natural History in 1897 as an assistant to Henry Fairfield Osborn. He travelled all over the world collecting dinosaurs and fossil mammals. Lots of Brown's discoveries, including the first specimens of Tyrannosaurus rex ever found, are displayed in the Dinosaur Halls at the American Museum of Natural History. Barnum Brown died in New York in 1963.*

Henry Fairfield Osborn *In 1891, the American Museum of Natural History hired Henry Fairfield Osborn as the first curator of the new Department of Vertebrate Paleontology. Osborn hired a talented staff of curators and collectors, including Barnum Brown. Osborn was responsible for identifying many new dinosaur species.*

Edward Drinker Cope and Othniel Charles Marsh *Edward Drinker Cope was born in Philadelphia, USA, in 1840. In 1884, Cope became the curator of the National Museum in Washington DC, USA. Othniel Charles Marsh was born in Lockport, New York, USA, on October 29, 1831. Cope and Marsh developed a rivalry which became known as the "Bone Wars". Between them, they identified 136 new species of dinosaurs, although many of these turned out to be duplications.*

William T. Hornaday *William T. Hornaday was born in Plainfield, Indiana, USA, on December 1, 1854. In 1880, Dr. Hornaday founded the National Society of American Taxidermists and, in 1882, was named the Chief Taxidermist of the National Museum (now the Smithsonian Museum). He later set up the National Zoological Garden in Washington DC, USA. In 1896, he became the first director of the New York Zoological Garden (the Bronx Zoo), which, under his supervision, became the largest and finest zoo in the world.*

Sue Hendrickson *In 1990, fossil hunter Sue Hendrickson discovered the nearly perfect remains of a Tyrannosaurus rex in the Black Hills, South Dakota, USA. Named Sue, after her discoverer, the 13-metre-long dinosaur sold at public auction for $8.36 million to the Field Museum of Natural History in Chicago.*

Peter Larsen *Peter Larsen, the director of the Black Hills Institute, South Dakota, USA, employed Sue Hendrickson, and sent her on a collecting mission in South Dakota, where the bones of a T. rex were found. Larsen quickly bought the rights from the landowner to excavate the dinosaur. However, a dispute arose which ended with Larsen going to prison for 18 months.*

Copyright © ticktock Entertainment Ltd. 2006
First published in Great Britain in 2006 by ticktock Media Ltd.,
Unit 2, Orchard Business Centre, North Farm Road, Tunbridge Wells, Kent, TN2 3XF
ISBN 1 84696 042 8
Printed in China
A CIP catalogue record for this book is available from the British Library.

CONTENTS

AN ACADEMIC RIVALRY

The 19th century opened with an unprecedented time of dinosaur exploration. Scientists and the public were very excited about the idea of ancient life that pre-dated mankind. Amongst the pioneers of the American West were palaeontologists and fossil hunters making new discoveries of dinosaur bones. The most famous fossil hunter of the time was Barnum Brown. Working for the American Museum of Natural History in New York, he had unearthed many dinosaur skeletons in Wyoming.

Barnum Brown

In charge of the fossils at the American Museum of Natural History was Henry Fairfield Osborn. As a student he was excited by finding his first dinosaur remains in Wyoming, USA.

AMERICAN MUSEUM OF NATURAL HISTORY

Osborn

When Osborn joined the museum in 1891 he vowed to build the best dinosaur exhibition in the world and gather the best fossil hunters around him.

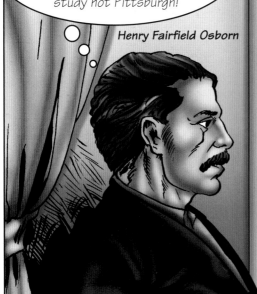

That steel millionaire Andrew Carnegie is building a new dinosaur museum in Pittsburgh. New York must become the centre for dinosaur study not Pittsburgh!

Henry Fairfield Osborn

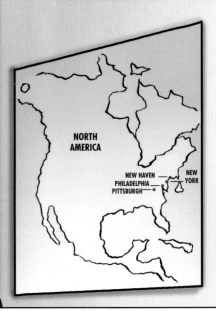

There were plenty of museums in North America during the 19th century, all on the East Coast. Osborn was particularly worried about a rival museum in Pittsburgh.

NORTH AMERICA

NEW HAVEN
PHILADELPHIA — NEW YORK
PITTSBURGH

There was a great deal of rivalry between museums over finding the best dinosaur skeletons, in the Mid West. For thirty years two scientists, Edward Drinker Cope of Yale University in New Haven and Othniel Charles Marsh of the Academy of Natural Sciences in Philadelphia, had competed with each other to make the greatest fossil discoveries. Their rivalry was dirty and became known as the "Bone Wars".

Edward Drinker Cope

Othniel Charles Marsh

Cope and Marsh poached workers from each other's expeditions, and stole each other's finds.

They violated treaties with Native Americans to expand their prospecting territory.

They dynamited their excavations when they were finished so that the other would not find anything left behind.

They even redirected each other's train loads of fossils to their own institutions.

Cope

Marsh is jealous of my knowledge.

Cope and Marsh pursued their rivalry in academic papers and in the newspapers.

The "Bone Wars" did not cease until Cope died in 1897 and Marsh in 1899. Their hurried and sloppy research damaged the image of palaeontology for a long time, but while at the beginning of the "Bone Wars" only nine species of dinosaur were known, at the end there were over 130.

My team of fossil hunters have made discoveries that Cope can only dream of!

Marsh

FAST FACT The three dinosaur periods are the Triassic, the Jurassic and the Cretaceous. Most dinosaur fossils found by the end of the 1800s were from the Jurassic period. Only plant-eating dinosaurs were known from the Cretaceous before Barnum Brown's work.

One of the best specimens in Osborn's collection in the American Museum of Natural History was the *Allosaurus* that had been found by Othniel Charles Marsh.

Allosaurus was the big meat-eater of the Jurassic period. There must have been a big meat-eater in the Cretaceous period as well.

Allosaurus

We must send Brown out west again. He must find more big dinosaurs, before Pittsburgh gets a better collection than ours.

The "Bone Wars" were not over! The American Museum of Natural History ordered Brown out on a bigger expedition.

THE FIRST SIGNS

In 1900, Barnum Brown was back prospecting in Wyoming, this time investigating rocks dating from the Cretaceous period. Near a place called Seven Mile Creek he made a discovery.

SEVEN MILE CREEK

This jaw bone looks exciting, but there is not much here. Wyoming is not really the place for Cretaceous remains.

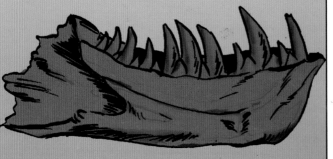

Brown packed up the jaw bone, along with a string of neck bones and a few ribs, and sent them back to New York. There were also pieces of fossil armour next to the jaw bone.

When he was back in New York, Brown talked to William T. Hornaday, the director of the Bronx Zoo, who had picked up some fossils while hunting in Montana.

Brown

Hornaday

This is definitely from a Triceratops, Bill. Where did you get it?

Out in the badlands of Montana. I have some photographs here.

That's it! That is big dinosaur country! That is where we should be looking.

FAST FACT When Barnum Brown was born in 1873 his parents named him after the famous circus owner P.T. Barnum, hoping that he would grow up to be as flamboyant and famous as his namesake. He did!

With no need for further discussion, Brown was off on another expedition. He took a train to Miles City, Montana, then began a five-day trek by hired wagon to Jordan, the place where Hornaday had found his fossils.

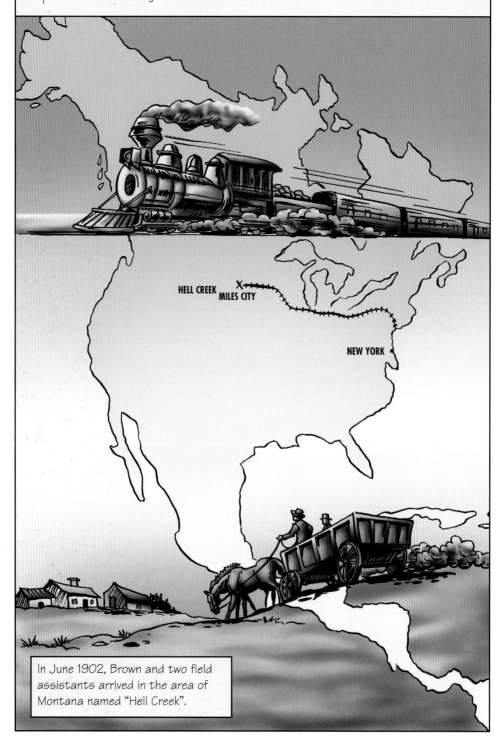

HELL CREEK
MILES CITY

NEW YORK

In June 1902, Brown and two field assistants arrived in the area of Montana named "Hell Creek".

As soon as they pitched camp, Brown and the team made their first discovery.

Look! There is something here all right.

But the rock up there is so hard. There is a Triceratops skeleton down here, and it will be easier to dig up.

Triceratops (right) was a horned dinosaur from the Cretaceous period. But it was a plant-eater – not what Brown was really after...

There is good stuff here all right. But I am sure I saw something really exciting up there. I have a feeling it is a meat-eater.

Triceratops

DIG!

PHEW!

At the end of the season the team began the 130 mile journey back to the railway at Miles City, bringing crates of *Triceratops* fossils, and part of the mysterious meat-eater.

There must be more of that meat-eater still in the rock. It will take more than three men to dig it out.

I should not have left it. It will weather away, or someone else will find it.

Brown was worried, however. He thought that a potentially precious find might be lost when the team left the site.

In 1905, Brown was back in Montana. But he was not in the area that he was interested in. Although he was in Montana, Brown was a long way from Hell Creek.

It's no good. I know that Henry thought that I would find good things in this area, but I have to get back to Hell Creek.

MONTANA

Brown decided to make the long journey to Hell Creek, but he experienced terrible problems. Torrential rain, the heaviest in Montana for years, slowed them down.

The horses were injured after being frightened by one of those new fangled motorbikes...

...and by the time Brown and his team arrived at Hell Creek, they found an expedition from Pittsburgh already working there.

Worried in case their rivals poached their site, Brown and his crew hurriedly extracted the rest of the specimen. They used dynamite to clear the overlying rock – a risky procedure.

Back in New York, Osborn received the new material and published his study on the specimen called AMNH 973, even though it was an incomplete skeleton. He had heard that Pittsburgh had found their own big Cretaceous meat-eater and was anxious to publish his findings first.

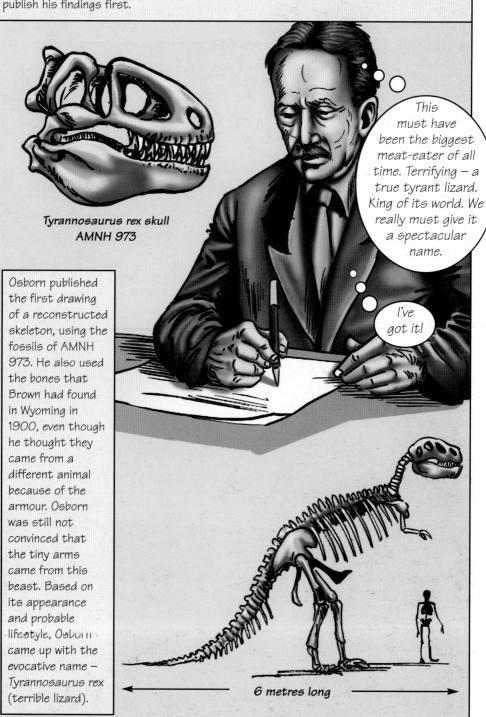

Tyrannosaurus rex skull
AMNH 973

This must have been the biggest meat-eater of all time. Terrifying — a true tyrant lizard. King of its world. We really must give it a spectacular name.

I've got it!

Osborn published the first drawing of a reconstructed skeleton, using the fossils of AMNH 973. He also used the bones that Brown had found in Wyoming in 1900, even though he thought they came from a different animal because of the armour. Osborn was still not convinced that the tiny arms came from this beast. Based on its appearance and probable lifestyle, Osborn came up with the evocative name — *Tyrannosaurus rex* (terrible lizard).

6 metres long

BACK AT HELL CREEK

Although the American Museum of Natural History had published the first scientific paper on the big meat-eating dinosaurs of the Cretaceous, Osborn was still worried that Pittsburgh would amass a bigger dinosaur collection for its intended museum.

And so, in defiance of Osborn's wishes, Brown continued to excavate in the Hell Creek area. He remained there for several seasons. His decision was right, for in July 1908...

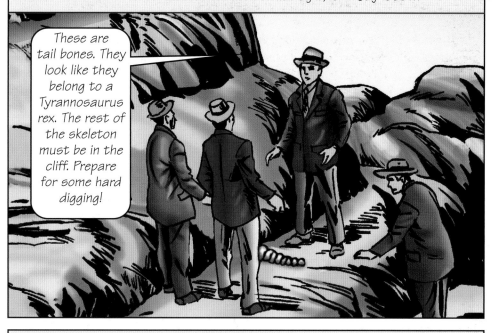

These are tail bones. They look like they belong to a Tyrannosaurus rex. The rest of the skeleton must be in the cliff. Prepare for some hard digging!

So Brown's team began the extraction of the next Tyrannosaurus rex skeleton – the one that was to be labelled AMNH 5027.

HEAVE!

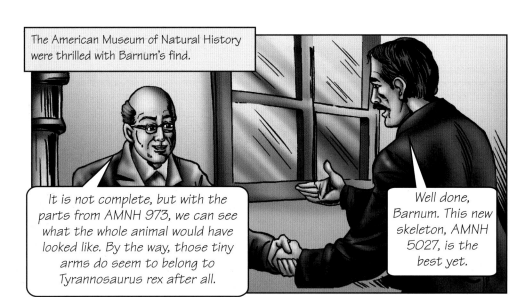

The American Museum of Natural History were thrilled with Barnum's find.

It is not complete, but with the parts from AMNH 973, we can see what the whole animal would have looked like. By the way, those tiny arms do seem to belong to Tyrannosaurus rex after all.

Well done, Barnum. This new skeleton, AMNH 5027, is the best yet.

Now the American Museum of Natural History had three specimens of Tyrannosaurus rex...

The first example, AMNH 5866, found by Brown in Wyoming in 1900, consisted of jaw, neck and a few belly ribs. By now Osborn had acknowledged that it was a Tyrannosaurus rex – the armour found with it had come from something else.

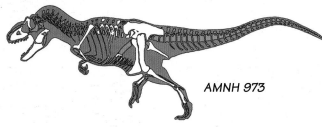

AMNH 5866

The fossils found of each specimen are shown in white.

AMNH 973 excavated by Brown between 1902 and 1905 is shown left. These are the specimens on which Osborn's original study was based. They consist of a skull, shoulders, hips and legs – and a few backbones.

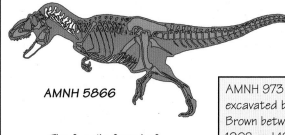

AMNH 973

AMNH 5027 was found by Brown in 1908. It was the most complete, lacking only the arms, the legs and the tip of the tail.

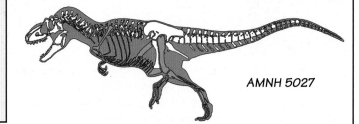

AMNH 5027

Along with the museum's illustrator, E. S. Christman, Osborn and Brown began to discuss how to display the magnificent specimens.

Brown

Osborn

Christman

We must mount these skeletons in the museum and show them off to the world.

We can make casts of all the bones, and make two complete skeletons out of them.

The first plans were flamboyant, picturing the skeletons of two dinosaurs posing as though fighting one another. A scale model was built.

Fine model, Christman. I can't wait to see the real thing assembled!

Just look at the size of it! That will never fit into our display galleries.

FAST FACT

Brown's original 1900 specimen was called *Dynamosaurus imperiosus* in Osborn's paper because he thought it was a different animal. If Osborn had mentioned that name first in the publication, it would have been used instead of *Tyrannosaurus rex* when it was realized that it was the same animal. We almost did not have the name *Tyrannosaurus rex*!

A PUBLIC ICON

It was finally **decided that the museum should mount only one skeleton.** This was largely that of AMNH 5027, but with limbs from AMNH 973. Because it was built from more than one skeleton, and there were some parts that had never been found, the mount was a little inaccurate in comparison to skeletons in museums today.

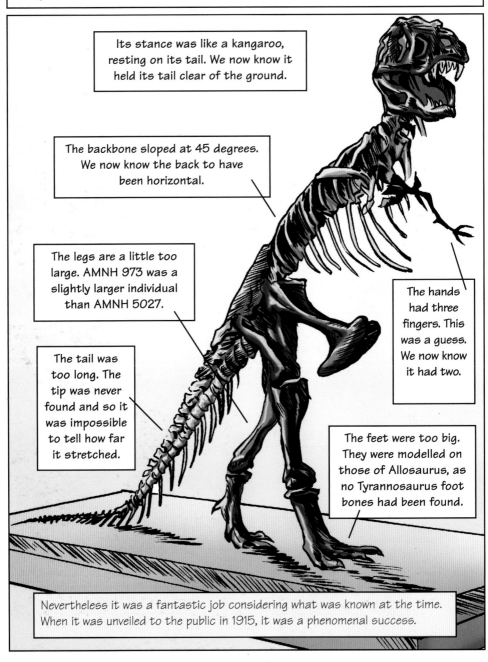

Its stance was like a kangaroo, resting on its tail. We now know it held its tail clear of the ground.

The backbone sloped at 45 degrees. We now know the back to have been horizontal.

The legs are a little too large. AMNH 973 was a slightly larger individual than AMNH 5027.

The tail was too long. The tip was never found and so it was impossible to tell how far it stretched.

The hands had three fingers. This was a guess. We now know it had two.

The feet were too big. They were modelled on those of Allosaurus, as no Tyrannosaurus foot bones had been found.

Nevertheless it was a fantastic job considering what was known at the time. When it was unveiled to the public in 1915, it was a phenomenal success.

The museum commissioned foremost dinosaur artist Charles R. Knight to paint a picture of what *Tyrannosaurus rex* might have looked like in life.

Knight's T. rex

Actual eye socket

Jaw muscles in here

Unfortunately, good as the painting was, Knight painted the eye in the wrong space in the skull. What he painted as the eye socket actually held the jaw muscles! This was the only time Knight made that mistake. His many later paintings of *Tyrannosaurus rex* all placed the eye in the correct place.

Tyrannosaurus rex – "King of the tyrant reptiles" – became a public icon. It appeared in books, comics, toys and motion pictures.

The most famous dinosaur film of its day was *King Kong*, made in 1933. It featured several dinosaurs, including a *Tyrannosaurus rex*. The *Tyrannosaurus rex* was based on Knight's painting in the American Museum of Natural History – it included the misplaced eye!

Tyrannosaurus rex

Between 1926 and 1930, Knight painted his most famous rendering of *Tyrannosaurus rex*, as one of the murals he produced for the Field Museum of Natural History in Chicago. This time he put the eye in the correct place.

In 1933, Chicago hosted the World's Fair. The Sinclair Oil company put on an exhibit of full-sized dinosaurs. The centrepiece of this was a *Tyrannosaurus rex* that was based on the Field Museum mural. It had a jaw that moved, and it made a noise. It was the first animatronic dinosaur.

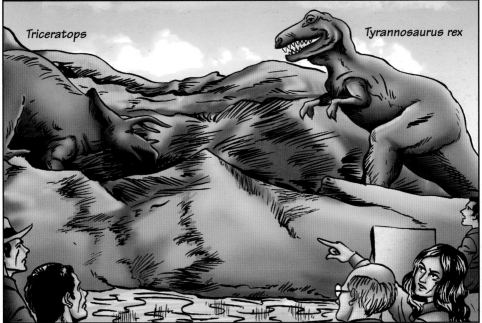

Triceratops

Tyrannosaurus rex

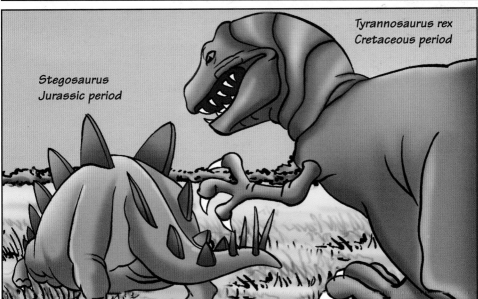

Tyrannosaurus rex
Cretaceous period

Stegosaurus
Jurassic period

Walt Disney featured a *Tyrannosaurus rex* in his 1940 film Fantasia. Unfortunately the film put T. rex in the wrong period, eating the wrong animals, and with three fingers on the hand, although by this time it was known to have had two. "It looked better like that", said the Disney animators!

In the late 1930s and early 1940s, World War II (1939 - 1945) swept across Europe. The famous dinosaur collection in the British Museum (now the Natural History Museum) in London became vulnerable due to air raids.

Precious specimens, such as this *Iguanodon* skeleton and sea turtle, were at great risk when bombs exploded near the museum.

Osborn died in 1935 leaving Barnum Brown in charge of the dinosaur collection in the American Museum of Natural History. When WWII began, Brown was worried.

And so, after decades of rivalry, Pittsburgh gained its *Tyrannosaurus rex* (left). It was the original specimen on which Osborn had based his first paper.

FAST FACT Brown was right to have been worried. In 1944, a bombing raid knocked down the Bavarian State Museum in Munich, Germany, destroying the only specimens then known of the meat-eating dinosaurs *Carcharodontosaurus* and *Spinosaurus* – dinosaurs even bigger than *Tyrannosaurus rex*.

Barnum Brown retired in 1942, and died, aged 90, in 1963. By then the curator of the American Museum of Natural history was Ned Colbert. In 1960, the dinosaur department in the Museum was reorganized.

We must do something with the first Tyrannosaurus rex skeleton that Barnum Brown found in Wyoming. I wonder if London would like it.

FAST FACT Edwin (Ned) Harris Colbert was one of the most important palaeontologists of his day. He found and named many new dinosaurs. One of his most famous studies was of a mass of little meat-eating dinosaurs called Coelophysis found in Arizona, USA. Colbert discovered the pack of dinosaurs had died of starvation in a drought, and had ended up eating each other.

Brown's first *Tyrannosaurus rex* specimen (still sometimes called *Dynamosaurus imperiosus*) became the basis for the *Tyrannosaurus* mount in the British Museum (The Natural History Museum) in London. It was the first time a *Tyrannosaurus* skeleton had been mounted according to modern ideas of its pose.

Head held well forward on neck with an S-curve.

Backbone held horizontally.

Tail relatively short and held well clear of the ground.

Tiny two-fingered hands with palms facing inwards.

Back in New York, the old upright stance of AMNH 5027 (see page 24) continued to be the major influence on how the public saw *Tyrannosaurus rex*.

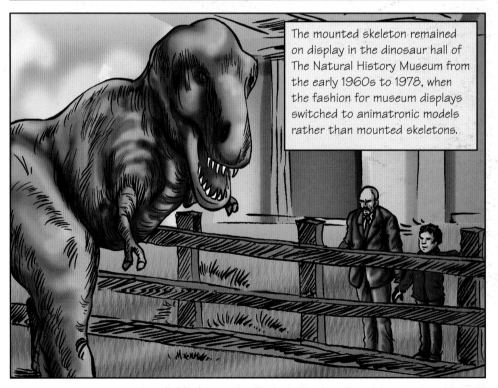

The mounted skeleton remained on display in the dinosaur hall of The Natural History Museum from the early 1960s to 1978, when the fashion for museum displays switched to animatronic models rather than mounted skeletons.

DISCOVERING SUE

The *Tyrannosaurus rex* story was far from over, however. In 1990, an expedition from the Black Hills Institute of Geological Research – a professional fossil gathering company – was exploring the badlands of South Dakota, USA, when their truck developed problems.

You guys go into town and get it fixed. I will stay here and start searching for fossils.

A member of the team, Susan Hendrickson, thought that the local area looked promising and stayed behind to have a look.

Dinosaur bones! This looks good.

It soon became obvious that the find was very important. The director of the Black Hills Institute, Peter Larsen, struck a deal with the landowner, Maurice Williams, to allow the Institute to excavate the fossils.

As the excavation progressed, the team became more and more excited. This was going to be the most complete Tyrannosaurus rex ever discovered.

Often a well-preserved dinosaur skeleton lacks the specimen's head. This one however, had an almost perfect skull. The skull was embedded in rock. So back at the laboratory of the Black Hills Institute in Hill City, Peter Larsen and his brother Neal, along with the rest of the staff, carefully dug the skull out of the rock.

And so the town of Hill City prepared itself to become a major centre for dinosaur research.

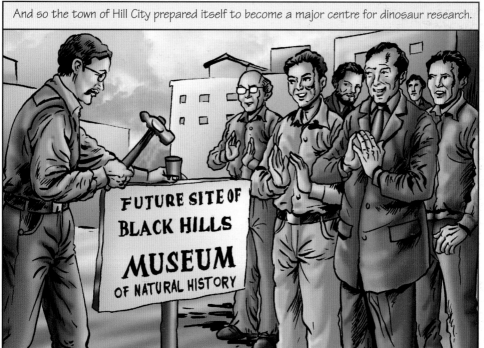

All was going well, until, on the 14th of May, 1992, the Black Hills Institute had a surprising visit...

Stay where you are! In the name of the Federal Government we have a warrant for the seizure of all fossil remains of one Tyrannosaurus rex dinosaur skeleton commonly referred to as "Sue". You have no right to it!

The skeleton had been found on a Sioux (Native American tribe) reservation. The federal government decided that Maurice Williams (the landowner), although Sioux himself, had no right to give the Institute permission to excavate the fossils. The government decided that it had been collected illegally on federal land.

The army confiscated the skeleton, taking three days to remove ten tonnes of remains. By that time the people of Hill City were up in arms!

Federal agents confiscated the Institute's papers, but had no sympathy from the townspeople.

The issue was political. The government wanted to stop people hunting for dinosaur bones for profit on federal land. The Society of Vertebrate Palaeontology – the governing body of dinosaur science – adopted this as their official line. Many leading palaeontologists disagreed.

Only academic scientists should be allowed to hunt for fossils. And there should never be money involved.

Nonsense! The Black Hills Institute may be commercial, but they are good palaeontologists and make their finds available for study.

A widespread popular campaign was waged, to try to get the government to release the fossils.

Meanwhile the specimens were lying under guard in a cellar. The storage conditions were far from ideal. It looked as if the fossils were going to decay beyond repair before they had a chance to be studied.

Finally the matter came to court. The issues about collecting on public land were so complex that they could not be decided. Instead, on 31st January, 1996, the authorities convicted Peter Larsen on currency irregularities related to the international sales of fossils by the Institute.

Peter Larsen served 18 months of his jail term.

Eventually, the Federal Government decided to auction Sue on October 4, 1997, at Sotheby's in New York. The Field Museum in Chicago came up with the winning bid after only eight minutes' bidding. Backed by funding from *McDonald's* and *Walt Disney World Resort*, the Field Museum won the auction with an astonishingly high bid.

The staff at the Field Museum then set about unpacking and preparing what turned out to be the biggest and best-preserved *Tyrannosaurus rex* skeleton ever found...

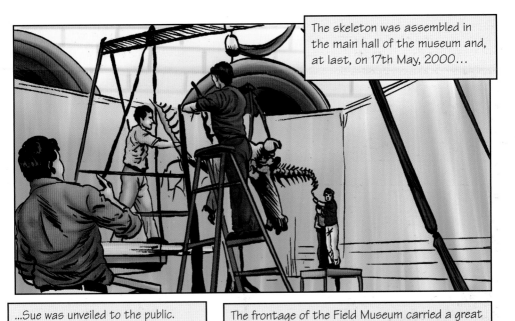

The skeleton was assembled in the main hall of the museum and, at last, on 17th May, 2000…

...Sue was unveiled to the public. The biggest and most complete mounted Tyrannosaurus rex in the world, Sue stands 4 metres high at the hips and is 13 metres long from head to tail. She is made up of over 200 individual bones.

The frontage of the Field Museum carried a great banner advertising Sue to attract visitors.

Sue

By this time, the media had accepted that *Tyrannosaurus rex* was no longer the upright, tail-dragging, slow-footed monster that previous generations had imagined. Famous presentations in the 1990s included …

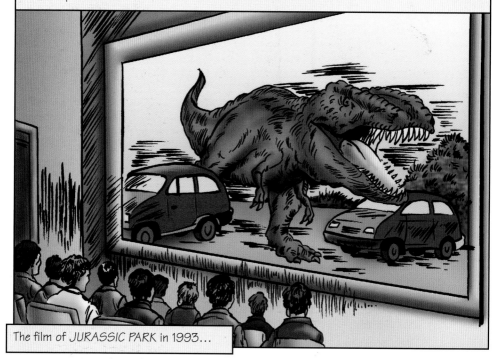

The film of JURASSIC PARK in 1993…

…the IMAX 3D presentation T. REX, BACK TO THE CRETACEOUS in 1998…

Argg!

...the BBC and Discovery Channel *WALKING WITH DINOSAURS* in 1999.

To complete the story, the skeleton of AMNH 5027 (see page 24) in the American Museum of Natural History was re-mounted during a major re-design of the dinosaur galleries in 1994. Now at last the *Tyrannosaurus rex* is in the tail-up, head-forward, horizontal back stance that is nowadays accepted by palaeontologists around the world.

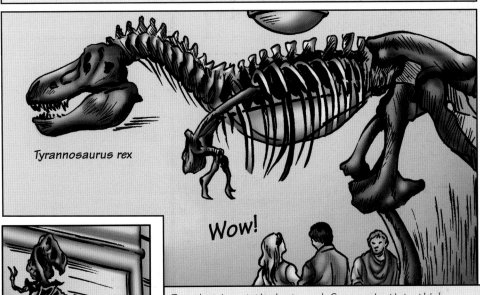

Tyrannosaurus rex

Wow!

But that is not the last word. Some scientists think differently. Bob Bakker, the palaeontologist who pioneered the idea of warm-blooded dinosaurs, regards *Tyrannosaurus rex* as agile and active. Bakker had a cast of AMNH 5027 brought to the Denver Museum of Nature and Science in 1990. He mounted the *T. rex* in a leaping, high-kicking pose, indicating a very acrobatic animal. There is evidently still much to find out about *Tyrannosaurus rex*!

TIMELINE OF TYRANNOSAURUS REX

 There is a long, long history that links the existence of a dinosaur like Tyrannosaurus as a living breathing animal, to the mounted skeleton that we see in museums today. This timeline gives just a snapshot of the geological, scientific, political and administrative issues involved.

68 million years ago: *Tyrannosaurus evolves, probably from a smaller member of the tyrannosaur family.*

65 million years ago: *Tyrannosaurus and all the other dinosaurs become extinct. A tiny proportion are buried and become fossilized.*

65 million years ago to present day: *The preserved Tyrannosaurus skeletons are buried deeper and deeper. As the surrounding sediments turn to rock, their bones turn to mineral.*

1822: *In Oxfordshire, England, Megalosaurus is the name given to the first dinosaur to be discovered.*

1842: *British anatomist Sir Richard Owen invents the term "dinosaur" to cover Megalosaurus and two other fossil animals found in England.*

1877-97: *The "bone wars" rage between Edward Drinker Cope and Othniel Charles Marsh. This opens up the Mid-West to dinosaur exploration.*

1891: *Henry Fairfield Osborn, curator at the American Museum of Natural History in New York vows to establish the best dinosaur exhibition in the world.*

1900: *Fossil hunter Barnum Brown finds the bones of a meat-eating dinosaur in Wyoming.*

1902: *Brown finds more specimens.*

1905: *Brown returns to Montana to excavate the specimens. Osborn names the new animal Tyrannosaurus rex.*

1908: *Brown finds a more complete skeleton in Montana.*

1915: *The first mounted skeleton of Tyrannosaurus rex is constructed in the American Museum of Natural History.*

1940: *Barnum Brown, now in charge of the fossils in the American Museum of Natural History, sends a Tyrannosaurus rex specimen to Pittsburgh for safety during WWII.*

1960: *Ned Colbert, the AMNH curator at that time, sends the first Tyrannosaurus rex specimen (the bones found in 1900) to London.*

1990: *The most complete skeleton of Tyrannosaurs rex, nicknamed Sue, is found in South Dakota, USA, by Susan Hendrickson. It is excavated by the Black Hills Institute of Geological Research headed by Peter and Neal Larsen.*

1992: *Sue is confiscated and the Larsens are prosecuted on a variety of charges involving the legality of fossil hunting. The matter becomes a famous case.*

1996: *The Field Museum of Natural History in Chicago buys Sue for $8.36 million. Sue is the biggest and most complete Tyrannosaurus rex skeleton in existence.*

1 There have been about 20 specimens of Tyrannosaurus found. About six of them consist of reasonable portions of the skeleton. This makes it one of the best-known of dinosaurs.

2 The Tyrannosaurus specimens were all found in the American states of Montana, South Dakota, Wyoming and Texas, and the Canadian province of Alberta.

3 A Russian relative of Tyrannosaurus, called Tarbosaurus bataar, is believed by some palaeontologists to be a species of Tyrannosaurus. If so, it should be called Tyrannosaurus bataar. This would extend the area in which Tyrannosaurus lived from North America to Asia.

4 There is still much that we do not know about Tyrannosaurus. In particular there is an on-going debate amongst scientists as to whether Tyrannosaurus was an active hunter or merely a scavenger, feeding on the bodies of animals that had already died.

5 It is likely that the young of Tyrannosaurus were covered in feathers. We know that ancestral members of the group were small animals that were insulated by feathers.

6 Bones are not the only remains found of Tyrannosaurus. There are coprolites – fossil dung – that are full of bone fragments from plant-eating duckbilled dinosaurs. These show that duckbills must have been its main prey. There is even a skeleton of a duckbill that has a bite out of its backbone shaped like a Tyrannosaurus mouth. Tooth marks in the bones of a Triceratops show that Tyrannosaurus must have fed on this dinosaur, too.

7 A single footprint has been found that has been attributed to Tyrannosaurus.

8 Dinosaur bones do not consist of the original bone material. Over millions of years the bones have been converted into mineral, as the sediments in which they were buried are converted into rock.

9 The mounted skeletons we see in museums rarely consist of the fossilized bones that were dug out of the rock. Usually technicians have made replicas of the bones in some lightweight material, just for display, so that the originals can be kept for study.

GLOSSARY

agile: *Something that can more quickly and easily*

Allosaurus: *The biggest meat-eating dinosaur of the Jurassic period.*

American Museum of Natural History: *One of the foremost natural history museums in North America. It was founded by Theodore Roosevelt, Senior in 1869 in the old arsenal building in New York city. The current building at 79th Street and Central Park West was started in 1874 and reached its present extent in 1936.*

Animatronics: *A form of robotics in which realistically sculpted animals or human figures are moved by mechanical means. The art-form was pioneered by Walt Disney in the 1950s, and was used in theme park displays and in cinematic special effects.*

Badlands: *An area of dry eroded gullies that were originally "bad lands" to cross.*

Barnum P.T.: *(1810 - 1891) An American showman who founded the Ringling Brothers and Barnum and Bailey Circus. He was famed for his over-the-top presentations and elaborate hoaxes.*

Bone wars: *The name given to the professional rivalry between Othniel Charles Marsh from Yale University and Edward Drinker Cope from the Academy of Natural Sciences in Philadelphia. Between about 1877 and 1897 they competed with each other to obtain the best fossil animal skeletons from the developing frontier lands – stooping to all kinds of low tricks to achieve this.*

bipedal: *A two-footed animal.*

British Museum: *Now known as the Natural History Museum in London. The museum was established as part of the British Museum in 1756 with the natural history collection of Irish doctor Sir Hans Sloane. The current building in South Kensington was completed in 1880 and the natural history department was separated from the rest of the British Museum's activities. The name was formally changed to The Natural History Museum in 1992.*

carcass: *The dead body of an animal*

Carnegie, Andrew: *(1835 – 1919) Scottish-American steel millionaire and philanthropist. With the riches he made in industry he established schools, libraries and museums, both in Scotland (where he was born) and in America where he lived. Amongst his most famous creations were the four museums in Pittsburgh including the Carnegie Museum of Natural History.*

carnivore: *An animal that feeds on meat.*

Christman, Erwin S: *(1885 – 1921) The principal artist and sculptor for the American Museum of Natural History, specialising in displaying life from the past.*

Colbert, Edwin H.: *(1905 – 2001)*
*American palaeontologist and curator
of the American Museum of Natural
History. His work was influential
in the widespread acceptance of
continental drift and its evolutionary
implications.*

continent: *Any of the world's main
expanses of land.*

Cretaceous: *The last period of the
Mesozoic era, 145 to 65 million years
ago. The dinosaurs were most diverse
at this time, as there were separate
continents with different animals on
them. It was the time of Tyrannosaurus.
The dinosaurs died out at the end of
the Cretaceous period.*

era: *A division of geological time.*

erosion: *The gradual wearing away
of rocks or soil.*

excavation: *The removal of earth
from an area in order to uncover
buried remains.*

Field Museum: *The natural history
museum in Chicago, established as the
Columbian Museum of Chicago in 1893
and renamed in 1905 in honour of the
donor Marshall Field.*

Hornaday, William T.: *(1854 –1937)
An American zoologist who pioneered
numerous conservation measures,
including the protection of the American
bison. He was appointed director of the*
New York Zoological Park in 1896.

Jurassic: *The middle period of the
Mesozoic era, 208 to 145 million years
ago. It is the time when the dinosaurs
expanded and established themselves.*

Knight, Charles R.: *(1874 – 1953)
American artist, regarded as one of the
greatest illustrators of dinosaurs and
other extinct animals. He worked for the
American Museum of Natural History,
The Field Museum in Chicago, the
Natural History Museum of Los Angeles
County and many others.*

Palaeontology: *The study of ancient
life. Note that there are two spellings.
"Palaeontology" is the spelling favoured
by European countries, while
"paleontology" (without the second "a")
is the preferred spelling in America.
A scientist who studies ancient
life can be a palaeontologist or a
paleontologist.*

Triassic: *The earliest period of the
Mesozoic era, 245 to 208 million years
ago. It is the period in which the first
dinosaurs appeared. All the Earth's
continents were joined together at this
time and so the same dinosaurs lived
everywhere.*

Triceratops: *The biggest of the horned
dinosaurs that existed at the end of the
Cretaceous period.*

Tyrant: *A cruel ruler.*

INDEX